EURASIAN MAGPIE

RED-BILLED CHOUGH

HOODED CROW

EURASIAN JAY

WESTERN JACKDAW

CARRION CROW

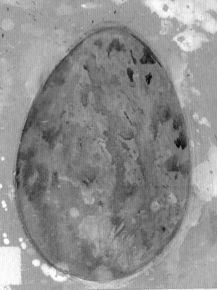

ALPINE CHOUGH

ROOK

THICK-BILLED RAVEN

For Jago and Lowen
CB

For Arthos—may you always
remain inquisitive and curious
OLG

CANDLEWICK PRESS

Nowadays, we are lucky enough to look up so many things on the internet in a matter of seconds. But despite the illustrator hunting high and low, even this seemingly infinite resource was unable to yield an image of the Flores crow egg—that's how rare it is. So we have left this egg blank. The global population of this crow, found only in Flores, one of the Lesser Sunda Islands in eastern Indonesia, rests at around a mere one thousand birds. Perhaps one day, if we are careful, the Flores crow will thrive again, and maybe you will discover what the egg looks like. If so, you can color it in!

The illustrator would like to thank the many bird experts and enthusiasts who helped with research for this book, as well as the Western Foundation of Vertebrate Zoology and the Cornell Lab of Ornithology, whose marvelous collections were of great help in offering visual references for some of the rarer crow species.

Candlewick Press, 99 Dover Street, Somerville, Massachusetts 02144 ◆ www.candlewick.com
Printed in Shenzhen, Guangdong, China ◆ 24 25 26 27 28 29 CCP 10 9 8 7 6 5 4 3 2 1

CLEVER CROW

CHRIS
BUTTERWORTH

illustrated by
OLIVIA
LOMENECH GILL

Wherever you are right now, there's sure to be a crow or two nearby.

Crows live across the world—on icy mountains and in leafy jungles, and in hot deserts and crowded cities. Crows are great survivors!

There are more than one hundred types of birds in the crow family.

It's not hard
to spot one.

Crows are big
birds with big heads and
big beaks. Most nest in
large groups called roosts
because it's safer
to be in a crowd.

Crows often build their nests
from twigs. It takes about
twenty days for their
eggs to hatch.

Crows are easy to spot, but they're easy to miss, too.

Most of the time you might not even notice them.

Crows have lived around people
for a very long time. It's easier for them
to find food where humans are growing
and eating food, too.

Farmers often scare crows away
from their fields.

7

Crows have no rainbow feathers
to show off.

EURASIAN JAY

A few members of the crow family
have a flash of color in their feathers . . .

but most of the crow family
are plainer birds.

AMERICAN CROW

EURASIAN MAGPIE

COMMON RAVEN

And crows are not
fancy fliers—
they don't zoom like arrows
or soar like kites.
Crows just flap steadily on.

10

Ravens are the
biggest crows
and the acrobats
of the crow family.
They can even
fly upside down.

CARRION CROW

11

Caw Caw Caw Caw

Crows are not
songbirds, either.

Caw

Instead of singing,
crows croak or caw—
they sound like birds
with very sore throats!

Caw

W Caw

CAW!

Crows work together
and help each other.
They greet other crows,
warn one another of danger, and tell others
where to find food.

But one thing is certain . . .

If a crow looks at you with its small, round eye,
you can be sure it's thinking.

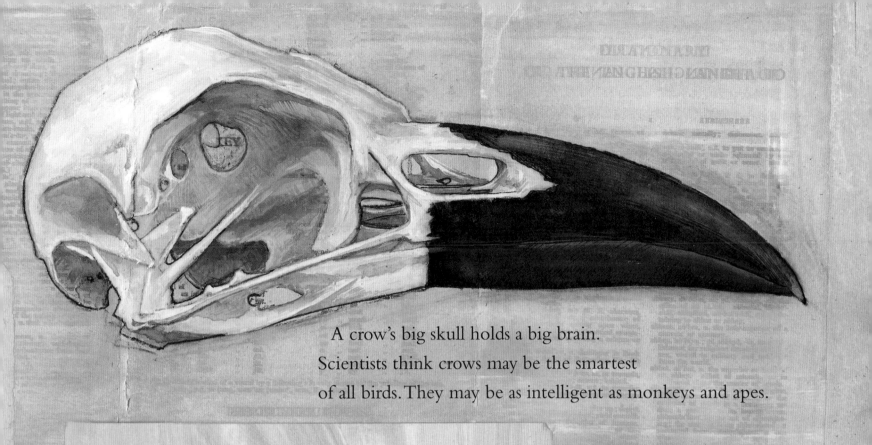

A crow's big skull holds a big brain.
Scientists think crows may be the smartest
of all birds. They may be as intelligent as monkeys and apes.

AMERICAN
AMERICAN CROW   AMERICAN CROW

Crows are clever birds.

Very clever birds.

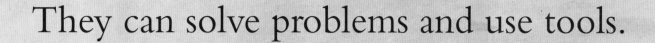

They can solve problems and use tools.

A crow will use its tough beak and strong feet to poke a twig down a crack and tease out tasty bugs.

Young crows watch
and copy the others.

16

Clever crow!

They remember things, too—

for a long time.

When there is food to spare,
crows dig holes to save some for later . . .
and they don't forget where it's hidden.

18

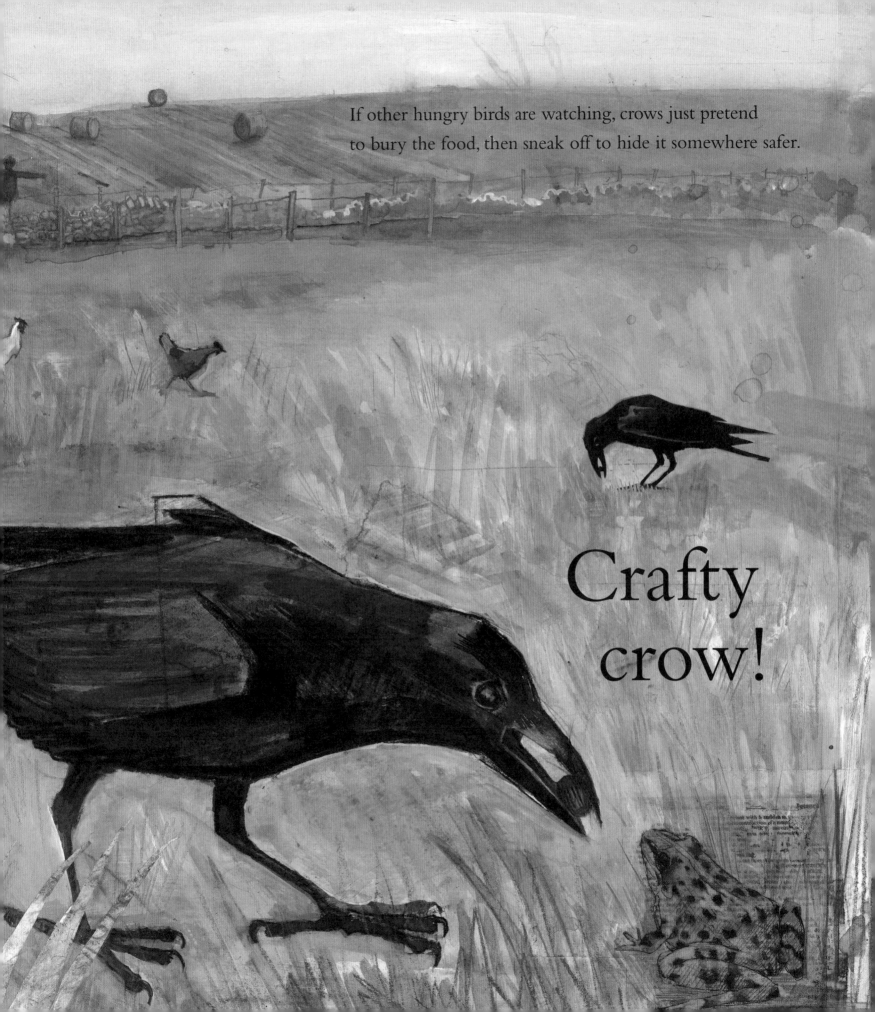

If other hungry birds are watching, crows just pretend
to bury the food, then sneak off to hide it somewhere safer.

Crafty
crow!

And crows know
how to play.

Catch them
in the winter
and you might
see them tumble
and roll down
a snowy roof.

Playful crow!

Play teaches crows
what to do in new situations,
but best of all . . .

it's a lot of fun!

Crows may not be graceful
to look at or lovely
to listen to.
But crows are smart,
clever, crafty,
and playful . . .

22

just like you!

Learn More About Crows

Crows like to live near people and other crows.

Can you spot any crows in the trees or on the streets near your home or at school?

Keep a notebook and write down what the crows are doing,
and draw some pictures, too.

Can you hear the crows cawing, warning the other birds of danger?

Are they going through the trash cans?

Are they hiding their food?

How are they flying?

How many crows do you see together?

And remember, crows are clever,
so they may be watching you, too!

Look up the pages to find out all about these crow things. Remember to look at both kinds of words: **this kind** and this kind.

Index

AMERICAN CROW

BLUE JAY

AUSTRALIAN RAVEN

CLARK'S NUTCRACKER

RUFOUS TREE PIE

COMMON RAVEN

FLORES CROW

FISH CROW

LARGE-BILLED CROW